Bedtime Stories for Kids

Short Stories of Animals for Children to Help Them Fall Asleep.

Sarah Mindfulness

Thanks to the simple narrative nuclei and situations of everyday life, this book offers the opportunity to listen to stories designed and written for children aged 6 to 9 years.
Small stories of animals, to let the imagination fly.

Upon using the contents and information contained in this book, you agree to hold harmless the Author from and against any damages, costs, and expenses, including any legal fees potentially resulting from the application of any of the information provided by this book. This disclaimer applies to any loss, damages or injury caused by the use and application, whether directly or indirectly, of any advice or information presented, whether for breach of contract, tort, negligence, personal injury, criminal intent, or under any other cause of action.

You agree to accept all risks of using the information presented inside this book. You agree that by continuing to read this book, where appropriate and/or necessary, you shall consult a professional (including but not limited to your doctor, attorney, or financial advisor or such other advisor as needed) before using any of the suggested remedies, techniques, or information in this book.

Table of Contents

Short Stories

of Animals

1- THE GLASSES

DISAPPEARED

A strange type of badger lived in the woods.

One evening he opened his eyes to get out of bed because he had forgotten to close the window.

She stretched and searched for her glasses on the bedside table. Nothing to do, there weren't.

-I'll do without it-, he thought and got out of bed. He immediately stumbled to the bed, ending up on the ground.

He got up, but not seeing well, didn't notice his slippers and stumbled ending up on the ground again, but this time he hit the wardrobe and dragged the chair on which all his clothes were resting on him.

Poor rate!

He told himself he would be able to get to the window to close it, but this time he gave the door a good head.

Without knowing how he found himself in the bathroom and with a somersault he ended up in the tub. It had completely lost its orientation and was full of bumps.

He decided it was time to ask for help to find his glasses, without them he felt lost.

So, she managed to get out of the house and went into the woods to look for friends and friends.

He met the owls but did not greet them because they looked like two seals to him.

He did not even greet the foxes, believing them to be unknown geese. Everyone started shouting: -The badger has no glasses, we must help him find them!

The badger recognized the voices of his friends and heaving a sigh of relief said: -Thank you, thank you very much, my friends!

They soon found them, and the happy badger was able to see his friends again. **Unity is strength!**

2- CLOVER SNACK

A rabbit comes out of its
hidingplace looking for a good snack

because it is tired of the usual clover leaves.

He sees a tablecloth lying on the lawn and curiously approaches sniffing the air.

How many good things are on the tablecloth: a bowl of salad, sandwiches, fruit, and bottles of milk.

The bunny is ready to start his snack when he sees a family of humans coming running with a hunting dog.

"Bau! Bau! Bau! ".

Immediately the rabbit runs away thinking: - Run my paws in search of clover!

The rabbit, taken by such fright, decides to be satisfied with the clover and never go near the tables set by humans again.

3- THE PIG ALESSIA

Once there was a pig named
Alessia who one day, looking at the
old mirror in the stable, found herself
in great shape.

She decided to organize a beauty contest with pigs and cows that are usually not considered cover animals.

Thus, she involved his female pig friends and cow friends, whose enclosure bordered theirs.

Contrary to popular belief, the victory would have gone to whoever was more fleshed out and toned of all.

Thus the participants began to eat healthy things, fresh things every day, and to take long walks around the farm.

Two cows gave up because they could not walk for long, three female pigs withdrew because they could not eat healthy meals, but were continually attracted by greed.

In short, Alessia remained, strongly motivated to win and to show that even pigs can be beautiful and two other friends.

Every day they walked together, every day they regulated their meals and encouraged each other not to give up.

The big day came and the four female pigs presented themselves in front of the bull, judge of the competition.

Indeed, the results were visible in all four female pigs and he could not make up his mind.

So, after thinking about it a few days, he decided that the beauty contest had been won by all three because they had given correct dietary and health rules, but a recognition was given to Alessia for having had the brilliant idea of favoring a correct style of life.

This beauty contest teaches that true beauty lies not in thinness, but in being healthy and fit.

4- THE COLORS OF

THE OWL

Once upon a time, there was a small and sad owl: its feathers were black, the legs, the beak, and eyes were very dark. He often asked his mother why it was all black and she replied: -

My dear, it means that nature wanted you that way!

The owl observed the other animals and felt sad: the butterflies had multicolored wings, the ladybugs were red, the grasshoppers green, the fireflies at night became bright.

He often asked the sun if he could hear his prayers and if he could give him some color, but he never got an answer.

But one evening, at sunset, the warm sun decided to grant the owl's wishes and give him two of its yellow rays: the first landed on its big beak, making it shiny, the second on the big and round eyes.

The little owl was now happy: it was no longer a single color. The day went into the woods showing all the gifts of the sun.

5- THE EAGLE AND

THE KITE

Once upon a time, there was an eagle that flew high in the blue sky.

Three eaglets took their first flight with her.

The little ones were not afraid to fly because they were with their mother eagle.

Aided by the wind, they flew over plains and mountains.

Suddenly they saw a strange bird with blue wings appear in the sky: it was a kite.

Mother eagle and her eagles flew together with the kite and the mother explained to them that it was not an animal, but a flying object that the children of humans use for fun.

After a long journey, the kite glided over the green lawn of a hill.

A group of children arrived immediately and happily greeted the eagle and the little eagles.

6- THE HEN THAT

FELT LIKE A CAT

In a small country town lived Nelly, a lady who lived alone in the company of her farm animals.

Nelly had a goat on her farm, three chickens, a spotted cow, pigeons (hard to say how many, as birds come and go), two rabbits.

The faithful Spino, an elderly hunting dog, helped her keep the troop together.

This story seems very ordinary, nothing strange so far, except for one of her hens. Yes, Serafina, the hen had shown some oddities from birth, ever since she came out of the egg, and instead of following mother hen, she followed Nelly in her housework.

She followed her and emitted a single chirp. Nelly was a little worried, she thought she had some health problems, but in reality, the chick was growing well and had become a beautiful hen.

Her oddities with time became continuous, but Nelly looked at her amused without worrying too much: when she was hungry the hen crawled on her mistress's legs, stroking her leg with feathers.

Her verses were now longer as if she were about to sing a song, and also there was no way to make her sleep in the chicken coop, she was always with Nelly and even landed on her legs, on the sofa, and even on the bed.

When she needed to go out to relieve herself she would stand in front of the back door and wait for Nelly to open it for her.

She was a bit spoiled, you might think, but Nelly had always treated her like a hen and decided that the next day she would talk to the veterinarian who came for the routine visit to all the animals.

- You know doctor, this hen is a bit strange! He has some really weird behavior!

- What do you mean by strange? - the veterinarian tried to investigate.

- Well, I could tell you that it acts like... like... like a cat, that's it!

- But don't talk nonsense, I've never heard such a thing in my entire life!

So, Nelly showed the doctor the oddities of the hen, who was amazed: he couldn't believe his eyes. He proposed Nelly:

-Every year there is a festival of exceptional animals, which do unusual things. Would you like to participate with your hen?

Nelly thought it would be a good chance to see the wonders our animal friends can do. In short, she signed up for the festival, Nelly and Serafina participated and.. ladies and gentlemen.. the hen won the first prize!

No one had ever had such a hen!

Nelly returned home satisfied and continued to have the company of the hen for many many years.

7- THE FISH SPARKLES

Scintilla had strange friends: the skier fish skied with two skis as if he were in the mountains, the sheriff fish wore the star pinned to his chest, he always chose it sparkling, the smooth fish was flakeless and knew how to glide perfectly between rocks and rocks.

Finally, the fish scarf was always cold and by dint of wearing woolen scarves, he had himself taken the shape of a scarf.

"What a partridge company! But are they fish?", Scintilla wondered every now and then as he slipped through the blue waters.

8- THE CAT SCRATCH

SHINS

A little girl had a cat that was always scratching her shins.

Sometimes the little girl would get blood and asked her mother if she put a band-aid to block the wound.

In this way, the mother always scolded the cat and he offended, always hid under the furniture.

One day the cat was so offended that he disappeared and everyone thought, not seeing him return, that he had ended up under a car.

After a few weeks the cat returned and having learned the

lesson, he no longer scratched the child's shins.

9- A LITTLE LITTLE

STORY

In the savannah, the sun rises
and in the cave the lion roars,

a leopard and three small leopards,
are struggling with two porcupines,

they spotted something far away,
four toucans on a banana tree:

they are three rather careless snakes

who ate burnt sandwiches,

two very rude parrots they make fun
of three obese buffaloes

and the crocodile in the hot mud open
your mouth wide to catch your breath,

and between two palm trees, what a
strange business, two kangaroos have
a snack.

This is the story of black Africa:
you decide: is it false or true?

10- THE YELLOW

WHALE

Many whales live in the ocean and one of them is special: it is all yellow.

The yellow whale is known to all the ocean fish that play with it every day. She likes to swim at the Polo and spends the summer among the hot islands.

One day he meets a strange fish. The yellow whale observes it for a long time: this fish is always above the water, it makes a strange smoke, sometimes a deafening noise and runs fast.

The yellow whale follows him to the coast and sees many other strange fish that make smoke.

The whale continues to follow that strange fish.

One day his friend dolphin notices this and explains to the whale that what he sees are not fish, but ships, boats that humans use to move on water and can be very dangerous for fish.

From that day on, the whale no longer chases the ships and watches them from afar.

11- THE BAT AND THE GHIRO

Once upon a time, there was a bat that had a bad habit: when it hung upside down in the cave to sleep, it kept its wings wide open and took up the whole place.

His companions were fed up and one day they went to ask the wise owl for advice: - Dear teacher, our bat companion does not understand that he cannot occupy all the place when we sleep, what advice can you give us?

The great wise owl thought about it and then came up with a great idea. The next day he accompanied the bat from the cold dormouse, who could not stand the drafts of his little house in the tree and was very worried because he could not rest well.

Thus, the dormouse and the bat came to an agreement: the bat could become a comfortable curtain that opened and closed in front of the dormouse door, protecting its house from drafts.

In this way the bat could open and close its wings as it wanted, occupy all the place it needed, without bothering anyone.

12- THE BEAR FAMILY

On a warm day, the mother bear walked with her young to the stream that flowed near their cave.

Mama Bear had dark brown fur, a pointed snout, an alert gaze, and two rounded ears that picked up on nearby dangers.

Her two teddy bears, two fluffy balls with protruding noses, were only thinking of playing and having fun.

As soon as she reached the stream, their mother immersed herself in the gushing water; the little ones remained to play on the shore when "Bum!", a shot made the birds of the forest fly.

The teddy bears realized that the hunters were close and desperately called their mom; around the bush had become silent.

The teddy bears were frightened: why did mom not answer?

Here, with a great leap, their mother reached them and began to push them quickly towards the cave where their father had arrived in the meantime.

The hunters approached the cave to catch the bears but the two large bears frightened them and made them flee.

13- RINO THE

RHINOCEROS

In the warm African savannah lived a rhinoceros that all the animals called Rino.

It was a big big beast, with four powerful paws and with a hard skin that, like an armor, covered it all.

On his forehead, he had a long, pointed horn over which was a smaller horn that not even he knew what it was for.

He was known by all for his temper; a trifle was enough to turn his mood black.

And then he looked around suspiciously and was ready to charge anyone.

Yes, because Rino, in addition to being irritable, was also quite bossy, he thought he was the biggest in the savannah.

One day there was an annoying air and Rino was more nervous than ever;

how he hated the sand that the wind made him get into his myopic eyes, he could already see little of it by himself! Suddenly a gust of wind stirred the branches of a tree near him.

The noise alarmed Rino who had his nerves on the edge of his skin, indeed his armor!

His little eyes saw a threatening shadow.

Who dares to attack the great rhino? - he snorted and without thinking he charged, running like a locomotive.

The collision was tremendous: the horn got stuck in the trunk and Rino give a head that was stunned for a few hours.

When he came to his senses and realized how foolish he had been, he was even more furious, but it took him two days to extract the horn from the tree.

14- TIMMY IN THE

MIRROR

For his birthday Paolo received a kitten as a gift, which he named Timmy.

This kitten is very special: he is convinced that he has a twin who follows him and imitates him in everything.

As soon as he passes through the corridor, his twin appears, identical to him, making exactly the same movements.

Timmy looks at him and his twin looks at him too, Timmy takes a step and his twin does the same, Timmy gets ruffled and there he is... the other cat does it too!

Timmy spends the day trying to understand why this other kitten always imitates him!

But can't he think with his brain?

And why does he always come out when he goes through the corridor when he goes to his mother's bedroom when he goes through the entrance?

He only sees it on these occasions, how strange!!!

Meanwhile, Paolo laughs, laughs out loud when Timmy is struggling with his twin, who knows why!

And you, did you understand who this twin is?

15- AROUND THE WOODS

It is October. A rustle is heard in the colorful forest: it is he, the dormouse, with his body made heavier by the recent feasting.

Acorns, walnuts, chestnuts, hazelnuts and berries-everything is gripped by those little fingers.

And then you see him gnawing and nibbling with relish.

Then he sits on a branch and with his little paws, he cleans his chubby face.

Usually he hides in the hollow of a tree, in the crevice of a rock or behind a bush and lazily waits for the night for his raids: he runs up and down the trees, from branch to branch, until he took what wants.

Now he is preparing his nest, stuffing it with moss and dry leaves.

When winter arrives, it will curl up there, with its tail around its head and sleep soundly, because the dormouse is a real sleeper.

16- THE WOODPECKER

LORENZO

Lorenzo was a young woodpecker who, together with his

father, mother and four other siblings, lived in a mountain forest.

Every morning his father took Lorenzo and his brothers to hunt in the woods.

Lorenzo did not like to wake up early and before he got up, his father had to call him several times.

Lorenzo did not even like to go hunting, he considered this activity too tiring.

He often invented excuses to stay with his mother and played around, flitting from tree to tree.

Time passed and our woodpecker fell behind with his dad's teachings, while his brothers were becoming skilled hunters.

How was he going to look after himself when his parents would no longer provide him with food?

Lorenzo said he would get away with it anyway: the thought of going hunting made him tired and he thought that tiring and difficult things were not for him.

One day, while his father and brothers were hunting, Lorenzo had remained at the nursery as usual, because he had found the excuse of a stomach ache.

Suddenly a large predator threatened to approach the nest, intending to eat the eggs that Lorenzo's mother was hatching.

The attempts of Lorenzo and his mother to chase away the bird were useless, so the young woodpecker left in no time at all to ask his father and his brothers for help.

He was going as fast as a rocket, he knew it all depended on him.

When they all arrived together, the predator was still around and Mom was very worried about the fate of her eggs.

Lorenzo, his father and his brothers chased away the predatory bird and Lorenzo was celebrated by everyone as "The savior" of his family,

because he had shown courage and
readiness in saving his family.

17- STORY OF A

KITTEN

Gigi once had a cute little kitten named Milo. He had arrived in Gigi's family when he was only two weeks old, because he had lost his family.

By dint of drinking milk, Milo had become a big cat: he was strong, alert and ready to shoot if he saw a mouse.

One day he managed to catch a little bird, but then he let it escape; another day he caught a white mouse, but then he let it go because he liked better the milk and cookies that Gigi's mother made him.

In short, Milo was unable to become a skilled hunter, as are all other cats, because he was too used to it and loved to rest, rather than get food.

In a few days Milo will become a dad: if you want a nice and cute kitten like him, but a little lazy, try calling Gigi's house.

18- MY DOG

My dog is nice
even if a little crazy.

He likes to tumble on the grass
and sometimes splashing around in
the water.

My dog is a Labrador
and he likes to play matador.

The electrician makes him bark

and the plumber runs away.

If they show him a cookie

he sits up instantly.

He likes company so much

of all, but especially mine.

He likes to be outdoors

mine is a dog to cuddle.

19- THE LITTLE FROG

GINO

Gino was a little frog who was in a hurry to grow up and do things like he was big.

The pond in which he lived was not very large and he wanted to see other ponds; it would take him a few minutes to reach the neighboring one, connected by a canal, where his friend Luigi lived.

Suddenly, however, it began to rain harder and harder, so much so that he had to take shelter, avoiding emerging from the water, in order not to get pinched by the big drops.

He took refuge under a large leaf floating on the water and waited for the rain to stop.

But for three days it never stopped raining and when the sun returned Gino noticed that the pond had grown enormously.

At that point Gino became disoriented: he did not find his home or that of his friend.

Gino was very sad, he continued to swim trying to find some face or known place, but nothing.

Gino was just looking for a place to hide and was so afraid not to go home.

At the bottom of the pond he saw a large empty shell and decided to take shelter inside.

One day his friend Luigi passed by who was looking for him and finally, hearing a friendly voice, Gino decided to get out of the shell.

With great relief, he hugged his friend and understood that there is a time for everything.

You cannot be in a hurry to grow up or to do the things that adults do.

20- THE GNOME AND

THE SPIDER

A gnome was sitting under a pine tree with his spider friend.

Their friends storks passed by
and invited them to go to a party with
them.

The spider said: -I can't come, I
have to finish my web!

Then the gnome proposed to him:
-I can help you!

And so the gnome and the spider
finished the web and then went to the
party.

The party was in a small house
behind the mountain. All the animals

had a great time and once they got home they went to bed to sleep and dream!

21- THE PENGUIN ALL MAD

There was a penguin who lived in the North Pole and he was a bit special: compared to all his other peers, he loved dancing!

He went to school and while the teacher was writing on the frozen blackboard he kept time with a paw, at recess instead of playing with his classmates, he delighted everyone with a ballet, when he left school in a single file he never missed the opportunity to do ballet before arriving in the arms of the mother.

Even at night, while he slept it could happen that the little penguin dreamed of dancing and the poor sister who shared a room with him, had to watch him as he lifted sheets and blankets in the throes of a dance attack.

One day his mother thought of taking him to the doctor, who only had to diagnose "acute ballerinitis", to put it simply, the parents had to accept the penguin as it was and indulge it.

Mom wisely thought of enrolling him in a dance school: there was no better gift for the little penguin!

There he could dance all afternoon and learn new steps, there he had fun and felt free.

Thus it was that the penguin was able to realize his passion.

22- THE RINO HORSE

Rino was a young horse who lived in the wild who loved having fun with his friends.

He was considered by these the bravest of all, because he was not afraid to go galloping in increasingly distant points, even far from the herd of adults, and then quickly turn back.

Rino, however, was hiding a secret that he dared not confess to his friends: he was very afraid of the dark. He was very ashamed of this and did not want it to be known.

The only people who knew about this fear were his parents.

Rino slept peacefully only when the moon was full or it was halfway through because in this way he was able to see around him and to give a name to the objects he glimpsed.

One day the young horse decided to go further than usual, exploring new grasslands and showing even more courage in front of his friends.

Suddenly they found themselves facing the ruins of an old farmhouse and curiosity drove them to sneak among the uninhabited rooms.

Some of the group mates pulled back, but Rino, trying to show courage, stood in front of the group and entered first, pushing the door with his nose.

As soon as he was inside, however, the door fell behind him, carrying bricks and beams from the ceiling.

Rino was blocked, he began to neigh with fright.

The companions comforted him by looking for other ways out, but it seemed there were none, so they decided to return to the herd of adults to ask for help.

Rino, after an initial moment of agitation, calmed down, thinking that help would soon arrive.

But in a short time the sky darkened and filled with clouds and the sky became dark.

Fear took over and Rino began to cry.

But he realized that the more he fidgeted and thought about the worst, the more fear took hold of him and took his breath away.

He decided to calm down, sit on the ground and wait.

He began to slow down his breathing because this made him calm down, he began to think about other things, about his runs in the prairies, about competing with friends, because this did not make him think of fear and soon he fell asleep.

He was awakened by the clatter of approaching hooves.

They were the adults, now he was safe.

They managed to move the rubble that imprisoned the young horse and Rino was soon free.

He learned a very important lesson: nothing happens to you in the dark, you just have to find a way to calm down and not think about it.

23- THE VALENTINE

CAT

Valentino is a black cat and lives on a farm. He enjoys playing tricks on other animals.

Pull the pig's tail, rip the feathers off the hens, jump on the soft sheep and nibble on the donkey's ears.

Everyone is tired of Valentino and his silly jokes. But he doesn't stop.

It scares the geese, chases rabbits, eats the farmer's wife's cake which has been left to cool on the windowsill and then dirties all the laundry hanging out in the sun to dry.

Then he goes home and happily drinks his milk.

But one day the farm animals decide to teach him a lesson: to scare him a little, they ask the neighbor's dog for help.

The dog Gianmaria was a hunting dog by now tired of chasing prey, but he would never harm his companions on the farm.

So, after yet another day of jokes and raids, Valentino returns home to rest: who does he find in front of his basket?

Gianmaria the dog, of course!

With a leap like a skilled hunter he launches on Valentino, who doesn't have time to defend himself, but finds an escape route in front of him.

Valentino runs, runs as fast as he can among the cultivated fields, until Gianmaria is no longer heard barking.

The farm animals watch the scene and laugh out loud.

After a few days, Valentino returns home cautious and afraid.

Surely the lesson has served him and from now on he will no longer bother his friends on the farm.

24- A STRANGE

READER

I am a special mouse, during the day I take naps where it happens, but at night I am very awake and full of desire to learn.

I certainly don't go hunting like all my peers.

My eyes have large pupils to see, and the light of a moonbeam is enough for me to read.

I learned to read pretty quickly and started devouring whole books! I am no longer enough short stories of a few pages, stories that I finish in five minutes.

I have been living in the library for a long time now and have grown accustomed to observing those who read books in silence and those who borrow them.

But a doubt arises every time I open a new book: will I be able to read all the books in the library?

25- A PIC NIC IN THE
WOODS

One day some very friendly animals decided to have a nice picnic in the woods.

The wise owl immediately recommended: -I recommend not to leave waste on the ground! Don't get the lawn dirty!

While they ate, however, they all forgot the owl's warning and between one laugh and another, between one song and another, the lawn was soon filled with garbage.

Suddenly a very strong gust of wind dragged all the rubbish into the stream! What a mess, now it was difficult to collect them all.

So they decided to organize: the birds in flight would use a large burdock leaf to collect most of the waste that ended up in the water, the beaver with a big dive would do its part and the squirrels above the branches would let fishing rods made with branches.

The wise owl, in the midst of the animals that were cheering on the banks of the stream, admired the collaboration that had been put in place and at the end of the "repair fishing" he congratulated everyone on the work done, reminding them that if they followed his advice shouldn't have worked hard to recover the waste.

26- THE CAT GIACINTO

In the quiet of an attic, Aunt Mimma's cat has crouched on a pillow in an old abandoned cot. That kennel soon became the home of five curious and lively kittens.

Mother cat takes care of her kittens, feeds them and fills them with licks. Among these kittens there is one who always has a tantrum, does not want to stay in the cradle and argues with loud meows. It's Giacinto, this fluffy kitten!

He has black fur, long whiskers that adorn his nose, two yellow eyes that shine in the darkness of the attic.

The four legs are covered with white fur and seem harmless: however, they hide sharp claws like those of an eagle. Giacinto balances himself on the edge of the cradle and throws himself nimbly into the void.

He wanders among the junk like an explorer. Enter the crate full of dusty books and notebooks, ambush a small rubber shark. Between jumps and runs he ends up in the bowl of water, getting his hair wet as if he had caught a shower.

His heart beats fast and his sharp meows bring Aunt Mimma to run. The aunt, with a lot of patience, dries it and then puts it back in its safe cradle.

Mother cat cheers him up by licking him from head to foot, but she is sure that Giacinto will still do something in about fifteen minutes.

27- THE TEO WORM

Teo was a worm who had nine brothers, he was the tenth, the youngest. Obviously he was the slowest of all, the smallest of all, the least intelligent.

Teo felt very insecure and the encouragement of his older brother who told him that he was not the worst, but that he learned last only because he was the youngest, was useless.

One day, Teo's brothers set out to look for food. Teo set off behind the brothers, but soon lost sight of them. At one point he noticed the shadow of a bird above him, intending to eat it, and immediately Teo sneaked into a hole in the ground.

Fortunately, the hole was narrow and deep enough to prevent the bird from reaching it with its beak, which gave up and flew away.

Teo, in an attempt to save himself, had snuck into Mr. Earthworm's house and when he noticed it he said: - Excuse me for the intrusion, Mr. Earthworm, but thanks to your house I'm still alive!

Mr. Earthworm complimented Teo: -You had a lot of courage, little one, do you know that it is not wise to go around and expose yourself to predators?

I congratulate you because you could have been paralyzed by fear, but instead you reacted by finding a solution.

Teo, encouraged by Earthworm's words, decided to join his brothers to prove to himself and to them that he too was capable of doing many good things and with a little time and patience he would be able to become a really good worm.